Praise for Cyrus Console

If you want new poets who speak to that history, who critique and confront it, then you will want Cyrus Console's majestic, aggressive, disturbing second book, *The Odicy* (Omnidawn, 2011). It is (as the pun in the title suggests) a broken-up, inside-out, postmodern epic journey, a fractured, frustrated attempt to discover justice, or purpose, or divinity, in our day.
—Stephanie Burt, *The San Francisco Chronicle*

This book contains some of the most distinguished prose poetry written so far in the United States. It is a book I and many other readers are likely to return to, a book whose stylistic virtuosity and intertextual richness never seem gratuitous; rather, they serve the cause of recovering a memory whose "episodes bleed from their contours, investing each other with error." Far from indulging in the metapoetic exercises favored by some representatives of the post-Language school, Console never hesitates to confront and engage with real objects in a way that is informed as much by Kafka and Beckett as by the lessons of contemporary phenomenology.
—Michel Delville, *Sentence: A Journal of Prose Poetics*

In a remarkable collection, Cyrus Console's "from The Ophany" stands out as a poem which immediately establishes its importance.
—Colin MacCabe, *Critical Quarterly*

Also by Cyrus Console

Romanian Notebook (Farrar, Straus and Giroux, 2017)

The Odicy (Omnidawn, 2011)

Brief Under Water (Burning Deck, 2008)

THE WAYFARER

Cover art by Corey Antis
https://cargocollective.com/coreyantis
Cover design by Lisa Maione
Cover typeface: Lydian
Interior design by Laura Joakimson
Interior typeface: Garamond

Library of Congress Cataloging-in-Publication Data

Names: Console-Șoican, Cyrus, author.
Title: The Wayfarer / Cyrus Console.
Other titles: Wayfarer (Compilation)
Description: Oakland : Omnidawn Publishing, 2024. | Summary: "Taking its
name from part of a lost triptych by Dutch painter Hieronymus Bosch, *The
Wayfarer* documents its speaker's attempt to forge a path through the
world – both as a father and as an artist – and to adequately capture the
experience of living through poetry. In language that melds the
vernacular and the archival, these ballads recall moments of love as
they arise in an everyday existence dominated by awareness of
political and ecological collapse. Caught between the terror of
wandering and the awe of witnessing new minds as they acquire early
words and memories, the poems hold out hope for the tenuous transmission
of meaning between generations."-- Provided by publisher.

Identifiers: LCCN 2024028597 | ISBN 9781632431561 (trade paperback)
Subjects: BISAC: POETRY / General | LCGFT: Poetry.
Classification: LCC PS3603.O5577 W39 2024 | DDC 811/.6--dc23/
eng/20240624
LC record available at https://lccn.loc.gov/2024028597

Published by Omnidawn Publishing, Oakland, California
www.omnidawn.com
10 9 8 7 6 5 4 3 2 1
ISBN: 978-1-63243-156-1

THE WAYFARER

Cyrus Console

Omnidawn Publishing
Oakland, California
2024

CONTENTS

THE WAYFARER

I was the father of two
Young children when I started
Plans for a long walk that became
Shelter in my mind where I
Arranged my things or chose
Among unlimited potential routes
Land and sky parting like
Content in a trance I could
Move west through

I had been made so
Any given morning brought
Regret I should be unable
To reverse progress out of sleep
Though both hands slept
Fastened around the black
Coffee that made me want to put
It all into writing but why
You know the taste

The thought of sleeping
Under bridges and drinking
Coffee there appealed to me
Autumn would have been perfect
I had a hat with a brim
Sandals that lasted forever
A knife and a steel bottle
I kept near the intercom
That relayed snores

The brain had certain templates
Representing less experience
Than the extinction of all
Alternative lines of descent
All futures not threading beige
Paths through wood and meadow
Not red fruit punctuating foliage
Not glittering sound of cool water
In which one beauty

Secret lay though it required
Talent sometimes to make sensible
Weird visual might of genitals
Outlines of predators and vermin
One kindred face upturned amid
Rent limbs and carnage
Thunderhead beneath whose mass
Crickets and owls gave out
Hesitant noise

For a long time I whispered
After my son as I covered him
Asked what a word was
Wanting to try to explain
The part of the secret that
Held there can be no first
Sight of such things
But my heart said only
Time to buy gold

During his first ice cream
Headache a look of understanding
Came over him I thought
Now one day maybe he can
Conceive a phrase like justice
System in the referral of pain
But it never kept me from working
The music I liked best was muted
So you could think

At summer's end big white
Mushrooms rose above the living
Mesh they were fruiting bodies of
And I had turned thirty-nine
Before I realized their names
Did not belong here
In the template of night
Is my water bottle a word
Is my pillow a word

One morning we passed under
Thirteen feet of chain sewn into
The hem of a hanging flag
On our way to meet a cartoon
Character who claimed to see
The same stars we could
And in the blue dark of Union
Planetarium he called us friends
And led us in a real song

CATCHMENT
CATCHMENT

That the children slept
In their beds through the night

And much else had not changed
But the vehicles and toys that made

Flight possible or the quaint
Metal slaves whose joints would whistle

As they extended and abducted
Five or so fingers in dutiful greeting

Were all of them dreams
No the future was a great

Listener and made many useful
Suggestions without ever seeming

To move from its place under the stairs
And I rode a bicycle to work

It was a mature technology
But I received looks now

Of what felt like contempt
Our employer required us to sit

As did our leisure
Children's literature carried on

Bravely the legacy of animals
Of the Mesozoic and Cenozoic eras

The nearest archaeological category
Would be the destruction layer

I refused a medicine that made
Crying difficult but reconsidered

The refusal daily for a period of years
From my pocket personal devices

Had begun communicating
Parts of what they overheard

To something with ontological status
That modified their content

I had not intended to say that
Move your finger please stop

Dad can you show me pictures
Of what people look like

When they are not living
Can we watch the bad guy

Who talks like a garbage truck
Did this dispense fresh water

For a price
Did this blow cold air

Was it mimicry
Is this the day we die

What is the anvil
The years permitted a surprising

Quantity of search space collapse
Later algorithms sort of laughed

And with a noise of pages sped
Onward into the vast content overhang

Where any twelve consecutive words
Identified a unique human speaker

War was other people it was going
To be sunny with a high of 114°

CURSOR MUNDI

If near the end of the level
The final resource is pooled
Behind hills in the flawless
Repetitive music of insects

Who live without metal to liken
Their pale sheeted heaven
And without interruption
And the soughing of a branch

Unweighted or the husked
Fruit tearing the canopy slightly
Once before striking damp turf
Does not break the appeal

Stranded in chemical time with no
Background apart from the period
Sound generally treated as silence
The whirring of a hidden fan

And the induction noise
Of data it keeps within
A narrow climate band which
Were they speakable would say if

You find yourself in a male body
Unable to believe you are still
Singing in October without hope
Of meeting a suitable partner

Let alone carrying out what
Work life has prepared you for
In the fumes the leaves run on
In the narrowing daylight

In that wonderful time
When liberation from the shame
And trouble of having confused
The role of philosopher with

Another role yet to be named
No longer seems improbable
In the late thirties
Just as the grammatical

Boundaries begin to line up
With the metrical ones
And you linger to pick twenty
Dollars from a dry fountain

Having destroyed the wise
Sayings by writing them down
Having filtered two images
Of nominally different views

Through disposable color lenses
Vaulted canyons and fired
Missiles on snake-like enemies
You might as well stop

For nothing because
The resignation you hear
Is not in the song
It is in a bone with six

Holes for music
Blood and scented flowers
A bone with holes for eyes
One for the will to issue

Downward a command like blow
Little sequence if you can blow
Free this arrow of white light
From the brow of a favorite child

CHILD ETUDE

By what dispensation does
The voice welcome us
To each new state

Unable to spell synthetic
Music without music unable
To write without music

Larding the script with it as if
To say music changed the sound
Of it and other words to music

Whereas legal said no magic
Words no magic outcomes
No measure yet appropriate

In a purely volumetric sense
To express the terrific sadness
Of having spent so much time

Maybe it was one but
The simulation was all we had
And in speaking the word

Simulation one conjured
That veridical outside which
Alone might conclude it

"They were made for singing
And no for reading but
Ye hae broken the charm now

POLAR EXPRESS

This is the beginning it begins with
The better parts of unrelated stories
The visual imagination shows quite abnormal development
Unquote in the treacly piano variations for a journalist
Whose form has appeared several stories below
There is a moment where the right hand
Seems conversant with the image of a small
Child hitching up its pants it
There is a hitch in the melodic line
Corresponding to the hand's movement
Chill wind in a tongueless bell
Hung on a tassel of dyed skin

Now the child is tumbling like its path
Could not contain the wish that started it
Prompting a rapid upwelling of dark love
For which the observer is unprepared
Season creep is a climatological effect
First observed in winter seasonal music
Dating from a period spent by the form
Wandering lost in the uncanny valley
Roughly from the advent of 64-bit platforms
Some say to this day unquote
It's true one spends the morning half
Listening to speech neither live nor inorganic

Now it is beginning in earnest unquote
The wetness and irregular texture
If one can call it that of the white
Of the hero's eye provokes a visceral

Unquote he suffers a crisis of faith
In an overnight delivery system
At first it seems impossible to believe
1931 is the first musical number
A locomotive corrected to the age of steam
With state-of-the-art tracking and surveillance
Capabilities unquote built in 1931 none of them
The voices is quite real

The child in desert pajamas has boarded
A quiet car adjoining the club car
The lost ticket buckles like a leaf
In the aquiline tread of snow
The sound of its crystals at the window
Like hot tea sugared in a metal cup
The dream if it is one might be said
To have an upper bound whereon
A man of the type called hobo squats
At a fire of the type called gypsy unquote
Boiling adult drink whose surface of incidental
Long-chain oil inspires steadying revulsion

He drinks the coffee of the transient
But even this fails to sober him
No stimulant can brace him now
No quantity of snow crammed in
At the jersey's ripped chest with a sound
One knows well and agrees is made
No fervent prayer or careful thought
No pipe-smoke forced into the rectum
In many Romance languages these rides
With their escape into vast unquote
Riveted iron holds for anthracite have
Names equivalent to Russian mountain

As gravediggers employed by the railroad
To make the people on the other side
Of the medium feel more at home
Mislay a critical fastener worked
In soft yellow metal other than gold
The crush containing mostly children
Calls out in one voice unquote from beneath
The accumulation of tension to make it stop
The first truly problematic anachronisms
Are melismata saturating the next three solos
Sung even as they pull into the wizard's village
A barracks with sapphire chimneys

But first the final car is freighted with the inherently
Traumatic concept of the marionette the figure
Given at length to understand that spilling
All the truth and everything it knows
Is only the beginning of an unreleased story
Related in the form of prequel to its own
No its own must take the shape of the remainder
Of what might profitably be confessed
One hates every minute of this feature
Hates it that the feature made one cry
Though the genre forbids it one begins to feel
One of the principal children should die

Maybe that is the medication talking
Absently stroking through aspirin and fine print
As it leaves the system under guard
Lugging a shoebox of personal effects
Over the hideous mosaic of the entry
Nutsack torn on the point of a star
Presently like someone in a heavy coat

Dancing in a strobe light in a deserted park
Wizened laborers dance at the service
Threshold of a frosted house of pain
Their faces scraped without the consent
Of murderers from the murderers' database

At the core of one's being unquote the knowledge
These are the final minutes whose requirements
Only the strong imagery of war can meet
See the wizard himself now his cloak taking colors
From the toadstool whose toxins focus in the urine
Of beasts restrained only by the length of their names
You who believe in him then disbelieve
Become him and end by resembling him
Spill your artificial fires that swim to earth
On spasmodic gestures of a whiplike tail
What I will remember most of all unquote
Is my son raising his lost tooth into the beam

ADJOURNMENT

Very good no markings
In a workmanlike hand

Book of my poems
In a dead man's room

Provision for stopping
The game to rest when

Serious players retired only
To study and reflection

How once free
It is with their stems

Oak leaves divine
A way down

Through two kinds of time
The first and the others

By the leaves
By the time

You crouch there feeling
Good is not

More than a made
Phrase by your lights

But here the parts
Of speech are drawn

Up and mixed in the lungs
Where blood aspires

To the faculty of touch
And a warm indistinct

Flood of feeling
Enters the verse

Like the voice
Of a bassist who died

In his sleep and was buried
Next to his son

In the passage to come
Doing the service

Against a syncopated
Flow of hard language

Evocative of the outer
Phase of fading in and out

Small pellets of tissue
Paper relaxing to crowd

A glass of clean water
With crimson blooms

The satchel that used
To mean you were

Somewhere in the house
Combining with other effects

Beside a portrait
On a mantelpiece

In a rental space
What song is this

Oh dead man how
Can I credit you for dying

In a way that allowed
Me to imagine I moved

In cooler circles
Free to stay

Up all night sleeping
Two hundred districts east

Of the river climbing white
Walls through the pinhole

Cameras that were his eyes
Tracks in the snow

In the forest at the end
Of endurance turning

Out to be your own
All the friends I could say now

To myself all the friend
I lost to the needle

Shaking my head
Tugging my sleeve

Phrasing it differently
By your hand

By your leave
Holding down the key

Of one letter absently
Forging a chain of sorts

ETUDE PROCEDURAL

You wanted to know
What the process was

Like for me it
Was like staring into

Whatever it was all
Examples of turbulence shared

Motives no less real
Or spiral for that

They passed with lessening
Fidelity among sightless particles

In a massive imagination
Like diffusion of vulgate

Loanwords through soft tissue
So-called thumbprints formed

During the long fall
Of a falling star

Through sky whose hot
Vortices spent its iron

Into brilliant linear sparks

CHARLIE BROWN

This yellow shirt with the black chevrons
An assistant professor in Kansas City
Believes it holds inexpressible meaning
One morning he wanted to explain it
But his voice was a valveless instrument
Left over from the jazz trio that signified
The boundaries of each great episode
And when we realized we could not point
Him out in the classroom or call to mind
One article of his clothing we wondered
For the first time if this was only another
Of the stress dreams he continued to have
About us for the term of his natural life
Shuffling illegible rosters or trying once more
To strike the balance between levity and rage
Capable of holding us in our seats
Even as with expressions of disdain
Like the first kernels exploding into white
Doves above an extremely hot surface
Some of us rose and gathered our things

A real professor would solve the problem
By accelerating the frame of reference
Pinning us against the black upholstery
Of gaming chairs someone suggested
We purchase with our own money
Which the computer wanted to edit
From the background but couldn't make out
So bits of it appeared stuck to our faces
Like black candy at the carnival

Then the professor had a plan for us
Then we'd be in the professor's hands
Instead he pointed with his travel mug
And a length of black drink fell from it
Class was just this long disordered speech
He kept saying there was a message
Too big or earnest for the special to fly
But it smashed all the records and came in
Second that night I think after *Bonanza*
About a band of cowboys voyaging
Farther from home than any other men

NASA took no special pride in them
In fact not even really trusting them
They fueled the landing module only halfway
So if they tried to land it on this mission
They'd never rise or gather their things again
On this point the administration was transparent
Colonel Franklin had seen negatives
Of the unidentified flying object
Captured on his cinetheodolite
Colonel Schroeder cheated on his wife
They said "son of a bitch" on live TV
And were only there in the first place
Because of a general shortage of astronauts
And don't you forget it he added unsteadily
Raising the worried blanket to his lips
Pacing before the whiteboard in his mind
I saw some birdshit glint a single time
Through the sunny window as it fell
While into tiny cameras everywhere
Ironically we gestured "land the plane"

The surface of the moon and the black
Space reflected in silver Kapton sheathing
The command module that bears my name
Offer peace to all men of good grief
This or *Snoopy* is apparently
The only manmade thing orbiting the sun
The environment is not manmade
Not in the sense of having made it home
I don't need to look up what I know
About the pine tree in my heart
God has seen the tape 56 times
And believes he will live forever but the violent
Tremor in his hand troubles my face
If we are really here then our trajectory
Shows he is liable to make mistakes
My head looks like an ancient satellite
My beagle has eaten another razor blade
And achieved local notoriety
Father promises to take me hunting
Once the unforgettable music starts again

A MAN OF LIMITED

What a day to be overweight
All one has in the world
On a park bench in a park mostly
Consecrated to the needle
When I was fourteen the poet Cyrus Console
Was my best friend in the world

My stepmother disliked him because he was
Sensitive and decently intelligent
And his father a doctor
All my stepparents disliked him
Decent was a word I favored
To indicate moderate quantity

Though I did not realize it at the time
I had certain of my first
Sexual experiences with him
He realized it
His manner betrayed neither pity nor disgust
Just lowering a previous estimate

He was always pointing out things like Italian
Wall lizards or the AH-64 Apache I never
Saw myself because I lacked a name
He taught a bunch of us to smoke weed
I figured he would be a pothead forever
We all did

He taught me to speak in code
We planned to dedicate our lives to following
A jam rock ensemble called the Dead
But in August 1995 Jerry Garcia died
A crowd gathered to cry and smoke weed
In Kansas City and we were part of it

Cyrus Console for decades
He would seek out pornographic images
Of unshaved women in loose floral print
You could hear singing through his office door
Robert Hunter was a great lyricist
Though I didn't realize it at the time

I had the most expensive vodka
And two packs of Marlboro Mediums
I completed the study of law
One time at the firing range spent brass
Landed in the collar of my shirt
Leaving me this scar

THE DENIM JACKET

One half hour in May
2019 deepening as if
Expressive of a process
Like cancellation but
Undergone by storms
The green dominant in
Windows of the science
Library among several
Places I recorded this

How to say this green
Color rare in nature
Apart from one reaction
Having almost no chance
The green of leaves
In the streetlight turned
Last night as you slept
Bright yellow threshing fat
Segments of illuminated rain

I can't tell if it's my book
On consciousness or pictures
Of a dress gone viral
Being white gold to some
Blue black to others but
I need you to know in case
I have to part out
The earth tone quilt creeping
Under the deaf cabin

Whenever I spoke of
The hungry charging
Phones in the square
Twice-named dogs miming
Enclosures that were just
Correlation between property
Line and pain right here
In the neck the pain
My face expressed

Listening for the key to fall
From great music or reading
The play considered best
How it made drama
Represent failure to act
I was happy this way
Stylized weeping broke
Up content throughout
The northern ballads

Terms of lament betrayed like
Musicality across languages
The extremes touched because
Strength of feeling curved it
Given crayons now
Children draw screens
And you among them
Hands held out dumbly
Beneath a senseless tap

Toward midnight you cried
Out for a green coat I'm
Not sure we own but
I comforted you and went
Back to my room probably
The dream was in color
One quality of duty is
To remember it marks
The perimeter of waking

At the window there
I am again the green
More varied in motion
Leaves and needles alert
But unconcerned oh
Wow some pollen
Bearing structure in the pine
Opening now pale gold
Clouds the annual breeze

MOTETS

Why should it bother me
To hear them nearly
Match their singing

To the pitch of screws
The traveling choir
Whose joie may never

Come this way again
Though I leapt in the streets
Then

*

At their faces' mercy
They stare in belief
The children in transports

With you Paula I
Still have these moments
My voice slipping

They say there is a life
Vest under the seat
That we are now free

Perfume in testers
In the sense of canopies
In shops with no duty

In the space between spaces
In musics like odor
One wanders through

In the bottle the London
Water is still cold
Though this is Bucharest

*

The modes I prefer
Give onto landscapes
Passing smoothly at great

Faintly perceptible speed
Fields of blue wheat
Stand there vanishing

Image of white wind
Turbines on the slope
Silent because it moves

Over the crowded roofs
Calls the hooded crow
The cock's crowing fills

Cool arcades with grape
I think many men must
Have broken in this station

Where I heard them process
A fratricide last night
His unmistakable cries

*

Notes held by Germany
When I was single
"Country lane" had no referent

The second rose functioned
As metonym for the exit
Wound made by a lance

Raw-boned youth wringing
The tail of a balking cow
Hand over fist

A return to the endless
Line snaking my castle
Channels trod in white stone

Wind fetched 100 leagues
Through a breach in the wall
Over forest one had not given

To ransom a daughter
Or anyone else
For that matter

*

Tunnels and other voids
In which fear was
First reliably contained

Thistle and caltrop above
Blankets and night soil within
Six feet of concrete

Shot through with bar stock
Two beach views concentrated
Marvelously by iron sights

Mesh and coil remains
Of a stochastic trap for minnows
Based on the funnel

Strands formed of shells
Whole strata of skeletons
Plastic and sea glass

As fractions of land mass
Fuel compressed from plankton
Epoch compressed from fuel

*

At noon to cross the bright
Waste separating resorts one
Mile from the aerobic threshold

Drives conflicted as finely
Powdered sugar in the windpipe
Nudists peering down

From caves in the soft cliff
Ruined shoes washing ashore
Like this

THE MONARCH OF THE GLEN

The station approaching the second
Class passengers rise and breathe
Smoke and spirit hard enough
To take me back into that version
Of myself who died of those things
And was cured in the rafters
Two handfuls of orange maize
And a knife in the throat
Was my name day that year
You see this is the continent
Sometimes called the old world

Loc de joacă reads the gate of the
Play area I take it
Reserved for those wearing
A bracelet the combination
Restaurant hotel resort issues
Overnight guests and yet
Here we are climbing
Gangways or catwalks planked
Haphazardly around old growth
Exculpatory signage fluttering
Autumn in an ill place

Everything welcoming or funny
About these mascots bad technique
Has transformed into menace
A dry voice chants from holes
In the face of a fiberglass tree
At the end of a high road

Squirted from a tube
Some great hoof has churned
The limp grass into printed clay
Filling with slips of rain
Put out your hand

I put out the hand
That scarcely closes
Around the deep piled velvet
At the great hart's antler base
Thick hot veins run up
The back of it like seams
Even seen far off there is
No mistaking a dead thing
And there can be less question
Of a live one even a monster
Conditioned to approach the rail

CURIOUS GEORGE

Often I felt I understood
Something only until I tried
Explaining it to you
An American of European
Descent rounding the Cape
Loaded with blue pigment

It was 6:30 there would
Be many hours like this one
People thought underground
It was dark when beneath
Soiled crust the planet worked
A ball of incandescent ore

You were not precisely human
They described you as happy but
Having the fault in your name
Reclining on the soft earth
Tilted in its bed and tilting
Soon the fun would be gone but

For now even the workmen spilled
Lunch onto the lawn from steel
Boxes as they forgot themselves
We revisited the doctrine of taking
The good with the bad like gold
Diggers who learn the trick

Of rapid focus on alternate pupils
Sparkling the gaze that holds you
And who should this be but
Your friend the man
Whose house you were in
Whose house always won

*

To say some but not all perhaps
To say sometimes habitually had
Power to delay a child's formation
Of harmful stereotypes but
Here in your maze-bright eyes
Glittered the question of habit

I have given it up though now
And then I open the cut glass
The sandalwood lid and inhale
Tristeza or mosaic reprised as
Viruses of the kingdom Plantae
Oh those far castanets are lovely

Maybe this stanza or one like it
Had power to compel change
In the body and breath of some
Liable fraction of enthusiasts
Inducing that condition it named
And the name of it was yawning

No doubt about it the cool air
Washing the tense throat clear
Saliva springing from ducts
Called fragrant by the adept
Lungs stretched by fresh
Emphasis on the continual

Vacuum in the belly yes
I think if you care enough
About breathing some of you
Here will take a breath that
Catches itself and intensifies
Crossing the record surface

*

The birds yawn in the trees
Striking up something not song
Precisely yet able to express
Doubt about whether the eastern
Sky takes on color or light
You can stop yawning assholes

The alphabet has no zero
Syntax is not a well order
Every lyric the phrase permits
Is contained in the phrase
This is George
Where is it now George the yellow

Hat that contains you
Entirely like a habit or bag
Dark helm the fallen traveller
In spirits laid at the palm's foot
Cap of thought you left home for
In Africa not further specified

By tureen and cruet laid on white
Linen the man sat you down
On a dictionary before a hot supper
Fog tumbling from his thermos
Tryhard standing in a crib of gold
Wire and ultramarine the supple

Reins laid down along your spine
A gentleman of fortune he was
His tone was the clattering sound
Of vultures quitting a dead tree
His jaw opened with the quick
Loud fillip of a light switch

*

Now he glances at his watch
Catchlights in his eyes like game
You lack means to grasp or kill
Two pipes in the red wingback chair
Later you reappear in striped pyjamas
Manipulating your slippered feet

While the backlog crumbles into music
Too many layers deep laid like a plan
Or a cheek on cool travertine
Stupefacients glitter in his case
Lined with velvet the small necks
In the glass recalling the ether

Ampoules in the hospital down
Whose staircase you tripped
Meeting the incredulous stare
Of the angel whose appointment
With you was in a port city
Many days distant

Stay with me George
How many did you take
How many were there
Live fish twitter in the vomit
Of idealized brine streaming home
From your mouth to the quiet sea

Two sailors hold you by the feet
One like every other man smoking
A briar turned in the billiard style
You jumped ship flapping your arms
Do you not remember this it was
Long before you got arrested

*

This phone was dialed literally
When the firemen came they
Only called the police
One resembled a composite sketch
Of a fat man made in a lean year
His partner seemed on point

Of backing from the windowsill
With a hot pie into parting corn
But they were cut from one cloth
And in the end no people were hurt
Though loving you I'm bound to say
Earth reaching only to your navel

Would give everyone in our family
Plenty of time to reach the first
Responders working to free you with
Maybe one truly competent person
Among them already having written
Mechanical asphyxiation on her form

Though true competence is rare
There was a competent poet gone
Overboard in a chill dawn like that
A competent poet whose young
Daughter made a tunnel in the sand
For example and disappeared

Life is full of cool hidden threats
You said it yourself in the voice
Animators of your huge franchise
Gave you that was one long vowel
Variably inflected by a banal
Vocabulary just out of cry

LANA DEL REY

Light woke me up
What I fed grew

Some fun could curve
The time of day

It's possible we were
Confused by old turns

Of phrase or new
Tonal and melodic ideas

Well no class managed
Its song that year

No teacher could get
The file to play

*

I fell in love
It broke my heart

The sign said Summer
Breeze Fine Apartment Living

Like that without punctuation
I felt I knew

You from somewhere before
Moths filed into flame

My modest band awoke
To the mild abrasive

Action of flung sand
The image did not

Realize it was cropped
Then I stopped digging

*

When I was young
Each keystroke was bound

To a single note
When I was gone

Machines wrote lyrics more
Perfect than we could

Imagine or there were
No machines and whoever

Was there to sing
Might continue to feel

It a spiritual exploit
It broke my heart

I fell in love
I fell in love

Light kept me up
What I fed returned

THE WIRE

Though your talking points
Like a mountain stream

Ran clear and unchanging
It was two decades

I did not study
No I laid down

My head and slept
In a dark carrel

*

Certain verses are lost
Because the phone understood

Them as search terms
You taught me once

We delete everything it's
Still there only deeper

Legible in the particular
As against the oracular

*

There is no wonder
But the fresh green

Revealed where clear urine
Splashes the greater plantain

Clean of gravel dust
And no name for

The black funnel thrust
Into the awed dream

*

Forests their virginity gone
Approach the castle thanks

All the lunar energy
Fallen on striped land

100% of the energy
Produced here is wasted

I take my song
Chopped and screwed thanks

*

Still the voice catches
When stray balloons appear

Crossing the various sky
What red cursive legal

Tender smell of cocaine
Silence on tape sudden

Wham of body mics
Unclipped and set down

*

We stood and watched
Hot wind blown loud

Though a jagged slot
This is the best

Lavatory in the world
You said to me

Later you said Dad
Can I whisper something

*

Everything in the Communist
Era trains continued working

Long after it broke
Where the steel bowl

Narrowed to a mouth
Sped the blurred earth

It makes me happy
When I stream music

*

These are generous comments
But I won't continue

Because I am alive
My children between them

Thirteen man-years of joy
All the best songs

Written already in committee
Ok Google take note

*

Is this the air
You were calling for

For four fall days
Native trees looking like

Embers on a pike
Someone shouts look away

Brights on on Meyer
Freeze icons in prayer

*

When we party now
We release the funds

And watch them fall
Like sunbeams through Nyquil

A dead Western people
Who numbered in octal

The flowers of Mendocino
Someone shouts look alive

THE LIBRARY

"Look at your hands" was one
Critical teaching the book I had
From the school library offered
As soon as you knew what it was
Look at your hands in the dream

In order to open something
Theoretically like a door to willing
Progress through wherever we are
Sent by night to wander among
Known persons and composites

"Progress" fails to capture it
The promise was total choice
Peripheral highway modulating
Into pine needles and orchids
Among the objectives of dream

Once or twice in the immediate
Sequel to that reading I believe
I came to myself and looked
Down to see my hands
In what was still childhood

Since my priority was to fly
Though I found I couldn't rise
More than a few feet or travel
Swiftly or with precision
There is a lesson here

No margin can contain
Next I noticed certain light
Radiating through the glass
And it was tomorrow
The day I read no further

Often without waking I enter
Into something like suspicion
This must be it there is
Something I have to do
Else why am I floating

While I look my eyes come
Open and the room returns
To mind like a technicality
I breathe and there is only
This feeling of having known

OLD YELLER

Once the virus reached
The shore I felt
No better time would come

For you to have one
Despite being unequipped
To care for it long-term

So the kitchen filled with hair
And talk of dogs and books
About dogs like this one

Which I regretted reading
Aloud once the stern
Father shot a Comanche

Man in the yard in the text
Just ahead of my voice
So I kept it from you

Picking up a few lines
Down the page thinking
Guns in the house

Given early in life
To every boy are American
As venison squirrel

Black-eyed peas cornbread
Wild honey and hogberry jam
Vanishing into the polite

Visitor's maw until he casts
A shadow to the creek
Where mad animals gag

And you follow the shadow
Its hand on your shoulder
Its voice in your ear

It's your responsibility now
Son to shoot anything
That don't act right

By the time you become
A man every dog that's
Seen you cry is dead

For seven nights lying
Together we read and I
Regretted it would end

Often I feared I had done
Unintentionally and without
Being able to say how

Some animal harm
Causing him day after day
Of terrible suffering

Salted side meat washed
Down with branch water
Cooled in a skin bag

I feared I was low-down
Mean and of no account
Out in the live oak cutting

Long strips from a doe
To hang in a marginally
Cooler place like one

Side of a licked finger
Held still so long you
Can have no idea

It was asking a lot of a boy
To understand the first paragraph
As governing a world to come

When it said "He made me so
mad at first I wanted to kill him
Then later when I had to

Kill him" but I read it
Anyway as details I had
Known before I was allowed

To burn incense in my room
Came back like a rush of joy
How screaming in the post oaks

Bolting naked from the drinking water
Or chucking rocks in a sudden
Rage at slights against the dog

Little Arliss for example served
Mainly comic purposes
And could come to no harm

Though one of the slain
Pit vipers in his pockets
In a pile of shed clothing

Kept working its mouth
Well on toward sundown
And we could hear Mother

In windless night whose stars
Hate the thought of quantity
Battle soil from the laundry

But we had to go back
Under the circling birds
Into the brush because

Being as good as dead
Yeller must survive in order
To understand "no"

In part and "good"
To itch and beg and be
Afflicted with worms

To put a windpipe
Between the back teeth
Just playing around

And to strengthen
The effect at last
Of dying on you

His howl grown thin
As a distant parent
Fixing to drive home

Through the tall grass
What on earth Travis
No kin to me Travis

JIG

A tea called white
That tastes like snow
A force named weight
Casting no shadow
A one-winged seed
Caught in the comb
Of rooted blade
And knotted limb
Once I climb in
My bed again

A word or two
For how I feel
A symptom or
A song called reel
Across the fires
The landmass blows
And all the creatures'
Names we know
In stereo
The evening through

A part of life
Such as the lungs
Fear and relief
And other things
For the purpose
Of this song
All the children
Form a ring

The wolf a fang
The moth a wing

The line on hold
The runner come
The cavern hailed
The first long home
First dignity
First trodden fruits
Drunk willingly
Through undrilled flutes
In darkened booths
More tales than truths

My friend has said
Song began when
Voice decayed
In cave or canyon
Or whelmed in hell
A panic troop
Enlarged itself
With shout and whoop
Locked noise of boots
And allez-oops

A favorite novel
Of Defoe's
Consists of several
Numerals
The quaint tabular
Evidence
Of which the dead are
Exponents

Awake with a start
Sat up in the cart

Behind the hedge
Men go golfing
Under the bridge
Someone is coughing
Into my elbow
Uncontrollably
Into my window
Old lullaby
A butterfly
A homeless guy

Now they call it
Twenty-five
Who said six feet
To save a life
A breathing room
A window well
Homely fathom
In the soil
A study hall
A parasol

With dropped chisel
Noise of chains
And sugared diesel
With fragrance
Of witch hazel
White ambulance
Whose personnel
By time and chance

And find the veins
And wash the hands

Where they piled up
I could not think
A freezer truck
A skating rink
Then from the lake
Block ice was hewn
Hauled in to stack
The bodies on
Or was that in
Some other song

Back of the bough
Forking the clear
Air lifts me though
No tune is there
Where I am is
That what you meant
Where I spend most
And am most spent
A long past tense
An elements

Not thou with me
The crescent moon
Nor you with thee
The perfect sun
The century
Of the chief good
In poetry
Rhyming with blood

A word salad
A murder ballad

Terse but fluent
Enterprise
Without enjambment
Or surprise
No day content
To memorize
Just rapid movement
Of the eyes
And you were there
Dad was alive

THE RAG DEVIL

I saw him in the street he was the blue plastic bag of plastic bags
The poor man his tenant painted threats against three city officials
On the wall of his building which also read glioblastoma please help
My name is Teddy and this is my number

I saw him in the dull rainwater filling a defective streetlight
He was in the phantom limbs of wildlife at the last moment softly
Lifted from the right of way in the so-called City of Fountains
It was from the right he attacked the first of the city officials

Old concert footage he was of the kind with large asterisms
Made to appear in a drawn-out shot of some keyboard player
Soft-edged golden artifact revolving lazily like a brain event
But I was of my time and could not help falling in love a bit

What was he really was it just more plastic bags or was it the mail
Of golden polygons bound like protection about a man with no bed
Protagonist of an award-winning game based on nonverbal folklore
Who crooning through reeds makes away with the distracted child

He was the hoist balk that spoke to the unbearable weight
Of movables from that era when things were made to last
He was the song in the wings of the various insects apparently
Having gone on all night like an idea of reference

Once after losing my way not far from home I saw
His face suddenly in the lightning scar on a walnut
I felt the front of his body in the thrill of wind blowing transcripts
Like this one into the cracked screen of a burner phone

Six olive helicopters issued low over the floodplain in a wedge
Made from the various distances between them and more significant
Against the second city official he formed a wedge and with it
Drove low-information constituents two ways across the plaza

He was this sense of uncleanliness concrete as any animal's
The almost-pleasant feeling as the drugs of night wore thin
My bare stomach frazzled with organic solvents and my lungs
Smoked like a brace of trout bound in fragrant wands of fir

But I was always glad things had gone the way they did despite
The handle of my knife crumbling away while I watched the game
The firemen were bronze and continued to point through artesian
Jets the color of their noise toward that horizon I gained upon

For I had commissioned them and would always believe in them
My arms vanishing during the catch and pull phase of the stroke
The dock shrinking with all its details to nothing behind me
And when I reached the land I might run again

PIPPI LONGSTOCKING

It happened sometimes you asked me
To play with you or differentiate
Between black birds or help find
Three things wrong and I said no
Grackles sing like old springs or a clock
Falling down stairs I take it back
And said nothing for a mile and a half

The song more resembles
A characteristic noise that tin makes
The element when it is bent
A bar of tin will cry until it breaks
A child might grow unnaturally strong
Wandering alone among the deceased
Family's possessions in its house

Mr. Nilsson the monkey is represented
As clutching a tin cup with both hands
The porch where it is contented to remain
Shelters a horse with no name
When I was a child it was said
Such and such were the only nonhuman
Animals accustomed to grief or mourning

Pippi is about your age and like her
If ever you should need something
I speak here purely of commodities
There is a mass of white money
Understood as persistent in the solid phase
In a suitcase on top of the wardrobe
To which you may repair indefinitely

My legacy to you in a bubble economy
Together with the poems I want
You to consider as most significant
Among three hobbies I pursued
In a kingdom whose only valuable sectors
Work diminished and degraded utterly
And where you got free lunch at school

They threaten to stabilize in the mode of lament
I have been all your life overcoming
And which perhaps needs no explaining
The sea chest in the attic moonbeam
Discloses a sword and three pistols
And the nightshirt I wore in life
Which might be taken in for you

You are seven but children's literature
At present can no longer accommodate
Two small brothers hemmed in by flames
In the window of a high triangular wall
The quip children should never handle firearms
As you present Tommy and Annika with revolvers
Look the illustrator renders Nilsson as ink

With paper-white eyes not at all as it is done
The shower of sparks over the groaning crowd
The tramps wink at each other then enter
At nightfall through an unlocked kitchen door
I believe there is a reason for this though
Whether we have told ourselves a kind of lie
Or whether we imagine it all so clearly

As the temporary wound cavity lofted
By the slug traversing a schoolboy's belly
That it no longer moves us to laughter I can't say
Much that Pippi's world restricted to caricature
Has since crossed the valley into our own
Nilsson's water cup he drains and afterward
Places atop his head like a cap or crown

Unbraided for the coffee party
Red hair encircles her visage like a mane
A little radiation is unavoidable she says
Thankfully the disaster meant everyone
Was already under orders to stay home
By the time wildfires in the Zone of Alienation
And in the State Radioecological Reserve

Unfurled luminous soot over Europe
I believe everything happens for a reason
I do it principally to teach you to do it
But in Japan there is a vault of ice they need
To keep cool for three thousand centuries
If humankind is to go on providing meals
For my father the cannibal king

Though you may never exceed what you did
Without apparent effort as a child of six
If you keep at it you will be a real artist
Say to yourself money is a gas whose pressure
Is the average velocity of coins and it suffices
To rigidify structures of increasing complexity and scale
Say you regarded the Settergren family as real

Sister trying on surnames in a fine hand
Brother clasping and unclasping his birthday knife
Mother wiping clean the glass eyes almost
As dark as the circle of very black paint
Marking Father's nose as a tin pipe
Proper to the emotionally distant man
I believed there was a reason for this

And then this annoying thing had to happen
That he was blown into the ocean
And Pippi came into the house to begin
Waiting for him to return which was
A frame of mind that offered no way out
But which instructs a concept of bad faith
Evoking pity rather than contempt

It happened sometimes you asked me
To play with you and I said no
But this will be the last time
And these are the black shoes precisely
Twice the length of her feet
Which her father bought her in Santiago
So that you would have something to grow into

LAXNESS

It came to me later in the day
Walking the dog I'd decided
To put down because among other
Recent aggressions she had
Bitten the child of a stranger

I had to walk her to get away
From thinking about it and that's when
His name finally occurred to me
An acoustic image descending
The vowel scale from "likeness"

A man's adulthood contained so little
Of it that I took note of anything
Such as his book that made me
Burst into tears
In this tears resembled laughter

In books I had encountered scenes
Of people bursting into song
In *Kidnapped* Alan Breck kills four men
Then bursts into a Gaelic poem
Composed by himself on the spot

But there were few experiences like it
I tried to remember the landscape
Was bleak and the suffering relentless
The view made up for a great deal
Even before the ocean came into it

The father was mean but you forgot
Everything about him in time
Except what he did to his daughter
That and the reindeer he rode
Into the blizzard and through

The river ice trying to kill it
And I would say who wrote it
But was drawing a blank
As I held my weeping child
At 4 a.m. in the converted room

Blankness was the better place
I promised you the vet would find for her
And there was hope and solace in it
Like a lake famed for its monster
A long form made of lake water

And then I thought of likeness
And the dog bursting into flames
And the flames licking my hand

BROWN ETUDE

I saw colors but couldn't
Place where they began
Or begin to count them
Could be a rainbow yes
Too late to tell

My teachers wanted basic
Sleep hygiene even
Housing they just drove
Around in a van
Under color of law

Solving a type of mystery
Penlight eliciting
Nothing from the pupil
Nothing of substance
Reflected in the minutes

Yet like a charm
A word like suede
That meant to rise
From its rude bed
Of buckled limbs

Again
Bled out and flayed
Say in the pressured
Speech of hymns
What need be said

The author thanks the publications in which these poems first appeared:

Agradecidas Señas ("Motets," "The Monarch of the Glen," "The Wire," "The Library")
Brick ("Cursor Mundi")
Critical Quarterly ("Child Etude," "Etude Procedural," "Brown Etude," "Curious George")
Harper's ("A Man of Limited," "Lana Del Rey," "Pippi Longstocking")
Lana Turner ("Adjournment," "Polar Express")
Sprung Formal ("The Rag Devil")
The New York Review of Books ("Laxness," "The Denim Jacket")
The Paris Review ("The Wayfarer," "Catchment / Catchment")
Under a Warm Green Linden ("Jig")

photo by Diana Pălădescu

Cyrus Console is the author of *Brief Under Water* (Burning Deck, 2008), *The Odicy* (Omnidawn, 2011), and *Romanian Notebook* (FSG, 2017). Winner of Fund for Poetry and Fulbright U.S. Scholar awards, he lives in Kansas City.

The Wayfarer
by Cyrus Console

Cover art by Corey Antis
Cover design by Lisa Maione
Cover typeface: Lydian
Interior design by Laura Joakimson
Interior typeface: Garamond

Printed in the United States
by Books International, Dulles, Virginia
Acid Free Archival Quality Recycled Paper

Publication of this book was made possible in part by gifts from
Katherine & John Gravendyk in honor of Hillary Gravendyk,
Francesca Bell, Mary Mackey, and The New Place Fund

Omnidawn Publishing Oakland, California
Staff and Volunteers, Spring 2024
Rusty Morrison & Laura Joakimson, co-publishers
Rob Hendricks, poetry & fiction editor,
& post-pub marketing
Jeffrey Kingman, copy editor
Sharon Zetter, poetry editor & book designer
Anthony Cody, poetry editor
Liza Flum, poetry editor
Kimberly Reyes, poetry editor
Elizabeth Aeschliman, fiction & poetry editor
Jennifer Metsker, marketing assistant
Rayna Carey, marketing assistant
Kailey Garcia, marketing assistant
Katie Tomzynski, marketing assistant
Sophia Carr, production editor